CHARLIE CHAPLIN

by Pam Brown

Picture Credits:
The Bridgeman Art Library: 12-3 (Forbes Magazine Collection, New York), 16, 19, 20, 21, (Victoria and Albert Museum, London), 18 (Musée des Beaux Arts, Lyons); Michael Holford: 27 (all); The Hulton Picture Library: 7, 14, 15, 17, 32, 45, 54; The Kobal Collection: 4, 47, 53, 56, 57; Museum of Modern Art/Film Stills Archive, New York: 42, 50; National Film Archive, London: 10; Popperfoto: 33, 46, 58, 59; Rex Features Ltd: 41, 55, 60 (both); Retrograph Archive Collection: 35; © Roy Export Company Establishment: 8, 9, 22, 24-5 including inserts, 29, 36-7, 40, 43, 48, 58 (below); Frank Spooner: 30, 51 (Gamma).

The Publishers and author, Pam Brown, would like to extend a special thanks to David Robinson for his cooperation and acknowledge their indebtedness to his extensive original work in his biography *Chaplin, His Life and Art* (Paladin, London, 1986).

Published in Great Britain in 1991
by Exley Publications Ltd
16 Chalk Hill, Watford,
Herts WD1 4BN, United Kingdom.

British Library Cataloguing in Publication Data
Brown, Pam.
    Charles Chaplin – (People who have
    helped the world).
    1.   Cinema films. Acting.
        Chaplin, Charles *1889-1977*. –
        Biographies.
    I.   Title.
    II.   Exley, Helen.
    III. Series.
    43'028'0924

ISBN 1-85015-143-1

Series editor: Helen Exley
Editorial and End matter: Samantha Armstrong
Typeset by Brush Off Studios,
St Albans, Herts AL3 4PH.
Printed and bound in Hungary.

CHARLIE CHAPLIN

The star of silent films whose inspiration gave hope and laughter to the world

Pam Brown

EXLEY

Roberty

CHARL

SUPER FILM PARIS

ATELIERS SUPER Paris 8.ᵉ Cité Trévise

Born into the music hall

Charlie Chaplin was born Charles Spencer Chaplin on April 16, 1889 in London. He was the second son for his mother, Hannah – she already had a son, Sydney, when she and Charlie's father, Charles, married.

Charles senior was a music hall entertainer and although not one of the big names, he was doing very well. Hannah was also an entertainer. A wonderful mimic, she had a sweet, charming voice, but it was not strong. She lived in dread of the boos and mockery that she had seen drive performers from the stage and sometimes from the profession. While they were by no means rich, the music hall provided the Chaplins with a comfortable living.

Music-hall entertainment had started in back street drinking establishments where amateur artists performed a variety of acts that astonished, amused and delighted the public. The entertainers came from the same back streets as their audiences. It was a hard life, but for gifted, ambitious young people like Hannah and Charles Chaplin it was a chance of fame and fortune: better than being "in service" as house servants, or working in the grim factories.

By the late 1800s, music halls were in their heyday in Britain – there were more than two hundred, with thirty-six in London alone. At a time when there was no radio or television, it was no wonder that anyone who could scrape the entrance money together came to the music hall. It was a place where they could forget the hardship of ordinary life in Victorian Britain. They could watch fire-eaters and strong men, dancers and lion tamers, jugglers and trapeze artists, actors and magicians – and join in the choruses of the songs.

Opposite: A French poster of Charlie Chaplin as the Tramp. People all over the world could identify with the Tramp and his popularity was, and still is, international. Here the Tramp looks forlorn and lonely – one of life's losers. But, despite life's difficulties, he always won in the end – somehow becoming a symbol to the poor, the failures and the losers of the world.

5

A divided country

Queen Victoria's Britain was rich and powerful and her empire stretched right around the world. But as well as immense wealth, there was great poverty in the country. Slowly, things were improving – the rich were no longer terrified that the "lower classes" would plunge Britain into revolution as had happened in some European countries – but millions of people still found it hard to earn enough to keep alive.

Victorian London clattered with hoofs – hansom cabs, brewers' drays, coal cars, milk floats and the occasional crow-black pomp of an expensive funeral, all nodding plumes and mahogany, flowers and glass. The streets were full of life. Young women sold flowers and there were men playing barrel organs, with little monkeys sitting on top. Children played skip-rope and tag, marbles and five stones, or swung from the lamp-posts.

As Charlie walked the streets with his mother, he saw the most terrible poverty – bare-foot children, blind beggars, people huddled in doorways – but, as yet, it meant very little to him. His family was, for the moment, safe and secure.

Hard times

Between acts music hall performers were encouraged to drink with the audience, for the bars were where the managers made their money. Charlie's father did – and, like many another entertainer, he drifted from cheerful comradeship into alcoholism.

His drinking was slowly, but surely, destroying his marriage. Hannah grew more and more worried and afraid.

When he went to America on a tour with a theatrical company, Hannah found new friends. Among them was a very successful and handsome singer, Leo Dryden. He was attentive to Hannah and she lost her heart to him. Common sense flew out of the window. In August 1892, she gave birth to his son, George Dryden Wheeler. Until then, Leo Dryden had given her some financial help, but once his baby was born, he vanished from her life.

Hannah's marriage to Charles was over and now she had three children to care for. Charlie was three and a half, Sydney nearly eight. She had always been a loving, caring mother and she loved this baby as deeply as she did her older boys. They were poor, but at least they had each other.

Then, with no warning, Dryden reappeared at her lodgings, snatched up the six-month-old George, and left. Hannah could do nothing.

Her baby was lost, her life was in ruins, she had no income and no one to turn to.

All her old hopes were gone, but Hannah was indomitable. Without her, Charlie Chaplin would have become just one more child lost in the poverty of Victorian London.

Lonely and poor, Hannah turned to religion for comfort. She earned a little money by home nursing and making dresses for the ladies of her church. Like all those who fell on hard times in those days, her chief fear was that they would be forced by poverty to go into the workhouse.

Above: London Bridge in 1892; the city was a hubbub of activity. Victorian London was an industrial and busy place where the rich of society and the poor were thrown together. The narrow cobbled streets were alive with the smell of the foodmarkets, the shouts of the stallholders and the horse-drawn carriages.

7

Charlie's first appearance

There was simply not enough money coming in and Hannah had to do something. She was afraid of the unforgiving music hall audiences, but her talent was all she had to offer. In desperation she decided to go back to the stage. But all her worst fears came true: her voice failed completely.

Poor Hannah's struggles to carry on singing were drowned in whistles, cat calls and boos. She fled from the stage.

The manager, listening to the uproar, was desperate. He saw little Charlie standing in the wings. He was better than nothing. He grabbed Charlie's hand and led him to the footlights.

Charlie was five years old.

The sight of this small child staring out at them brought a shout of laughter from the audience: but Charlie had been brought up with professionals and performance. He planted his feet firmly and launched into a song.

The rumbustious audience was delighted and flung coins on to the stage, demanding another song. When Charlie calmly announced that he would go on once he had picked up all the money, there was another great shout of laughter.

The grinning manager assured him that he would see all the coins were collected up and Charlie carried on. He was enjoying himself and he went on dancing, singing and doing impersonations until Hannah carried him from the stage.

She was to give only one more public performance after that night – but for Charlie it was the beginning of a life in entertainment that was to make him famous all over the world.

Poverty

Gradually, Hannah was forced to sell all their small treasures – and then even the things they needed. Life could have been miserable if she had not brought magic to it. Their shabby room seemed to be transformed into a glittering stage. She sang and she danced for her little audience of two, and acted out plays for them. She told them stories from the

Bible that moved them to tears.

Somehow she not only managed to keep Charlie and Sydney clean and warm, clothed and fed, but she conjured up little treats for them – a weekly comic, the occasional herring for breakfast. Hannah's attempts to keep them decently dressed were not so successful. She concocted clothes from her old theatrical costumes and the boys were teased unmercifully as they went about the streets in their strange, oddly-cut suits.

Sydney was trying to earn some extra money by selling newspapers, jumping aboard the horse-drawn buses and racing up the stairs. One day, he found a purse on the empty, rain-swept upper deck. There was no name or address in it and it seemed

A photograph taken at the Hanwell Schools for destitute children. Charlie, aged seven and a half, is in the middle of the group – third row from the front, third boy in from the left. He spent part of his childhood in homes for orphans and destitute children. The homes were often quite modern and clean but for every child it meant forced separation from parents and an unfriendly atmosphere.

to be full of loose change. It was only when he got it home that Hannah discovered an inner compartment containing seven golden sovereigns.

Hannah decided to blow the lot on one glorious day out.

She whisked the boys off to the seaside on the steam train – to a day of shellfish, peppermint rock, cream buns, lemonade and fun ... with the lads in brand new clothes that had no hint of the music hall's "property basket" about them.

Such days of glory were few and far between, but when money was short, Hannah showed the boys how to find amusement without it.

She would sit at the window watching the passers-by and guess at their characters from the way they looked and behaved, spinning tales to delight Charlie and Syd. Sometimes she would mime all that she saw in the street below, her hands and her face describing it to the boys without one word being spoken.

Charlie took in her skills just as he took in the sights and sounds of London – and went on using them all his life. When he was a multi-millionaire and a world-famous actor, he would say that it had been his mother's skills and his story book childhood that had given him the perfect training for his career.

"It seems to me that my mother was the most splendid woman I ever knew ... I have met a lot of people knocking around the world since, but I have never met a more thoroughly refined woman than my mother. If I have amounted to anything, it will be due to her."

Charlie Chaplin, from "Photoplay", 1915.

The Norwood Schools

They were perhaps a strange little family, Hannah and her sons. It was as if they had built a sheltering wall around themselves, and now that wall was crumbling. Hannah began to suffer from frequent and violent headaches. They became so severe that she was forced to go into the infirmary for a month.

There was nothing else for it – Sydney had to go to the workhouse. From there he went to the West Norwood Schools for the infant poor. The schools were well run, and modern for their time, but they still had the stigma of being a charity institution. Sydney stayed there for three months and was then discharged into the none-too-competent care of Charles senior as Hannah was not yet well

The famous picture of Victorian poverty by Luke Fildes called "Homeless and hungry". It was memories of his own family's hardship that Chaplin drew on in so many of his films. Poverty like this gave Chaplin a passionate desire to see the underdog succeed and to fight against the injustices of the world. This was personified by the Tramp whose courage gave a lot of people hope and laughter in the face of their own problems.

enough to have the boys home.

Charlie had been sent to stay with relatives and got in a week or two of schooling, but he was never to have a real education.

When Hannah was well enough, the boys went home, but her headaches returned and once more she had to be taken back into hospital.

Another separation

The authorities were at a loss. Charles senior was quite well off, but would give nothing to support his children. There was only one thing that could be done. "Owing to the absence of their father and the destitution and illness of their mother" the boys were to be sent to the Central London District Poor Law School at Hanwell.

The rules of the school were strict. The boys

must be separated because of their ages. Charlie was now seven and Sydney eleven.

Sydney had been like a dad to his little brother and good food, playing fields and a swimming pool could not make up for their being parted.

The most miserable thing that happened to Charlie was catching ringworm and having to have his head shaved and coated in iodine. He felt like an outcast. Another disaster was when he was unjustly accused of behaving badly and was punished with three hard strokes of the cane. In his autobiography Charlie recalls feeling quite pleased with himself despite the unfair circumstances.

On January 18, 1898, Charlie, after eighteen months at Hanwell, came home to his mother. Two days later Sydney joined them. They were most desperately poor, moving from one shabby room to another, each more wretched than the last.

"I remember the Lambeth streets, the New Cut and the Lambeth Walk, Vauxhall Road. They were hard streets, and one couldn't say they were paved with gold. Nevertheless, the people who lived there are made of pretty good metal."
Charlie Chaplin, *talking about London, 1943.*

The Railway Guard, a typical London music hall character of the 1880s. The costumes on stage were simple so that the character was immediately obvious. Charlie's years as a teenager working in the music hall were the perfect training for silent films. He became a genius at miming – some thought the greatest in the world.

One day of freedom

It was not long before they were back in the workhouse and the schools. Hannah was not allowed to visit the boys, but she was not a woman to be beaten by rules. She told the authorities that she now had enough money to set up home again – and Sydney and Charlie were duly handed over to her at the workhouse gates.

They all set off for Kennington Park, a dreary patch of worn grass, whose only glory was a large municipal fountain.

Sydney had saved ninepence. After deep discussion, they laid it out on half a pound of black cherries, a twopenny teacake, a penny herring and two halfpenny cups of tea, all scrupulously shared between them. Sydney made a ball from newspaper and string and they played all afternoon, until Hannah said it was time to go home.

Back to the workhouse!

Hannah had no means whatever of setting up a new home. The authorities were appalled by her effrontery. There was nothing in the rule book to deal with such impudence. To their glee, the boys had to spend the weekend in the workhouse with their mother.

Only two weeks later, she was taken from the workhouse back to the infirmary.

The news was brought to the boys at the Norwood Schools. They were told that their mother, broken at last by her troubles, had gone insane and that they were to be sent to their father. It was a terrible and frightening day.

Moving again

They were taken to Charles' house in the bread van. He was living with a sad, devoted woman named Louise, but both she and Charles were often drunk and, as Hannah had declared, it was no fit place for two young boys. When Charles was sober, he was delightful – but he was rarely sober. The boys were terrified by the drunken rows, the shouting and the fights.

One evening young Charlie got back to the house

to find himself locked out. He did not know what to do. The morning seemed very far off and there was no one he could turn to.

To pass the hours away, he drifted about the dreary streets, keeping clear of the blackness of the alley-ways. Drunks staggered against him, couples brushed past, laughing and chattering. From open windows came the sound of babies squalling, of singing, of shouting. He felt desperately alone.

At last he found himself outside a public house, lights glowing through the frosted glass and the open doorway giving a glimpse of polished wood and shining brass. He lingered, envying the people inside the warmth and companionship.

Someone began to play a song on a clarinet.

The lonely boy listened, enchanted.

It seemed to him the most beautiful, reassuring sound that he had ever heard. These few moments outside a London pub opened his heart to music. He never forgot. One day he, too, was to compose tunes that were to delight the world.

An early photograph of a heavily made-up music hall artist. The make-up and clothes brought definition and excitement to the character, and the actions were exaggerated for better effect.

A proud moment

Hannah was an incredible woman. Somehow, against all expectation, she was well enough to set out, and, once more, make a home for her sons. They moved into a room backing on to a pickle factory and alongside the horrors of a slaughterhouse. The stench was memorable but they were together again. Charles even sent Hannah some money – probably to ensure that the boys were not sent back to him.

Charlie, most unwillingly, was sent to school. He was not very good at reading or writing, but he had one moment of triumph. His recitation of "Miss Priscilla's Cat" won him the applause of the entire school ... he was marched from classroom to classroom so that everyone could enjoy his performance. Suddenly he felt someone of value, not just one more shabby child.

But on November 25, 1898, Charlie left school forever. He was nine years old. His childhood was over.

The Lancashire Lads

Hannah was keeping the family together by doing outwork. Once a week, her employer brought round a pile of cut-out blouse pieces.

The pedal and whirr of the sewing-machine filled their days, for if Hannah fell behind she could not earn enough to pay the machine hire, or to live on.

Food was bought in tiny amounts, when they could afford it. The boys would go clattering down the steep stairs to fetch some pot vegetables and meat scraps for dinner, or a dab of pickles to cheer up some cold meat. A bag of stale cakes was a treat.

Sydney's wages helped. Quick and smart as ever, he was now a telegram delivery boy in buttoned uniform and pillbox hat.

Charlie knew he, too, had to earn a living, but his mind was made up. His upbringing had left him with no romantic notions about theatrical life, but that is what he wanted – to be an entertainer.

Life in Victorian London was full of hardship – whole families moved from one small room to another with few possessions, and little food. When the rent could not be paid, the threat of the workhouse and the orphanage hung heavily over their lives.

16

Charles senior was still in the business, although his drinking was destroying his chances of real success. He may not have excelled as a father, but here, at last, was something he could do for his son, and at no expense to himself.

He persuaded a William Jackson to take the boy into his troupe of child clog-dancers, the Eight Lancashire Lads. Because the group was out of the ordinary, it was proving a great success on the halls.

A stage apprenticeship

It was a lucky choice. Jackson was a kindly man who took care of his "lads", but insisted on a professional discipline and very high standards. It was excellent grounding for any future on the stage. Rehearsals, matinees and evening performances would leave the boys very tired, but they were professionals. Their job was to entertain – and to smile as they did it. If their dancing began to lack sparkle,

These children are not waiting to see a famous person or a music hall show – they are hoping for a free meal. Even if there were more people than there was food, it was worth waiting because there was no other way for many London children to get anything to eat.

The songs, the costumes, the exciting atmosphere ... the music halls took the audiences out of themselves and their miserable everyday lives. They were places to forget troubles and to laugh a little, just as cinemas were in the next generation.

Mr. Jackson was in the wings, gesticulating – and the smiles reappeared.

The Lancashire Lads shared the bill with some of the greatest performers of the day. Charlie stored away everything he saw.

Christmas was a riot of transformation scenes and flying ballets, glittering costumes and knock-about comedy. The demon king shot up from a star trap in a flash of red smoke, the Fairy Queen descended gracefully from above.

But Charlie saw, as he had as a tiny boy, the exhaustion and tension and the injuries behind the wonderful performances. He was part of a world that smelled of gin and greasepaint, dust and sweat, tigers and sea lions, gas and linament.

Charlie's first steps in the acting world had been very successful, but after only two years his days with the lads came to an end.

Now at night Charlie would sit and watch Hannah bent over her sewing, her fingers guiding the cloth under the relentless needle, her eyes red with tiredness.

The magical days of the stage seemed to be over for Charlie Chaplin.

Into the darkness

And now another blow fell. Charles Chaplin senior, destroyed by drink, died – aged only thirty-seven.

Sydney was away at sea and it seemed to Charlie that he must earn at least something to help out while his brother was gone.

He bought narcissi cheap at the market, made them into penny bundles and hawked them around the public houses. The mourning ribbon on his arm and his sad, dark eyes touched many a woman's heart and earned him a few extra coins – but his mother found out and put a stop to it.

"Drink killed your father and money from pubs will only bring us bad luck," she said.

But she kept the proceeds.

Cake and ice-cream

It was 1901. Charlie, aged eleven, was determined to find work. He turned his hand to anything – errand boy, doctor's boy, page-boy, and even glass-blower, though the heat was too much for him and he only lasted a day.

Sydney came back from sea with his pay and some money from tips – enough to transform the summer. Charlie was to say when he was older: "This was our cake and ice-cream period." Toasted tea-cakes, fish, muffins – the days went past in a

In the nineteenth century clowns came in a great variety of different costumes. The character in this picture is Scaramouche who, in many ways, is similar to Charlie's Tramp: he is vulnerable, sad and a mime artist. The same skills are common to both actors and the same feelings of pity and sympathy are felt for them both.

delicious dream, but soon Sydney had to go back to sea – and poverty closed in again.

Charlie tried selling their old clothes in the local market, but they were too dilapidated even for the desperate. He started making tiny wooden boats, but the glue endangered Hannah's sewing and the toy making had to come to an end.

Hannah was changing. However short money had been in the past, their lodgings had always been neat and bright, but now they were becoming more and more dusty and untidy. Charlie, not understanding, sometimes scolded her, but it was not apathy that was causing the change in her.

Illness again

One summer's morning, Charlie, weary of the drab cramped garret, went off to visit friends. About midday, he was sauntering home when some children stopped him.

"Your mother has gone insane. She's been round handing out lumps of coal and saying they are birthday presents for the children."

Charlie raced up the narrow stairs and found his mother sitting in her old place by the window. She looked at him with bewildered eyes.

"I was looking for Sydney. They are keeping him away from me."

Charlie had seen his mother ill before, but not like this. Charlie, fourteen years old, took her to the infirmary, walking the mile to the great iron gates with his arms around her as she staggered. Passers-by regarded them with disgust, for they thought her drunk.

In the high, bleak room a doctor calmed Hannah and gently examined her. He told Charlie that she was indeed unwell. Hannah was admitted to the infirmary and six days later to the asylum.

Alone

Not wanting to be taken into care again, Charlie told the officials that he was going to live with relatives. In fact, he went back to the empty room to live alone until Sydney came back from sea.

The shoeshine boy was a common sight in Victorian London: it was a way of earning some money. When Charlie was fourteen years old he was totally alone and destitute, but there were always odd jobs to be done for a coin or two. Charlie turned his hand to helping wood-choppers, to being a telegraph boy and to glass-blowing.

Hannah, as always, had kept the worst from him. He found some washing soaking, no food save a half-empty packet of tea and three halfpennies. There was a little bag of peppermints on the table that she had bought as a treat for him.

In the next weeks, Charlie wandered the streets of London, as lonely as he had been when his father had barred the door against him. Thankfully, he fell in with some friendly woodchoppers and worked for them. It was company and the boss gave him two pence to buy bread and a bag of cheese rinds.

When Sydney came home, the two boys went to see their mother. They were shocked to see the change in her. Away from her old familiar surroundings she seemed to have become utterly lost and bewildered. Charlie was haunted for a long while by what she said to him in her confusion:

"If only you had given me a cup of tea, I would have been all right."

The market place was the heart of London life. Busy stalls lined the streets and street sellers shouted out their wares as they carried them from house to house.

Charlie finds his feet

Charlie had always believed, even in the worst times, that he had something special locked away inside him. Now, shabby and poor, he was determined to make a new beginning. He plucked up his courage and went to see one of the top theatrical agents in London.

The clerk looked at the fourteen-year-old. He was very small, with delicate features, tiny hands and feet, a mop of curly, black hair and magnificent teeth – a very good looking boy, and somehow packed tight with energy. He put Charles Spencer Chaplin on his books.

Only a very short time later a postcard arrived at Charlie's lodgings. His heart pounding, he went to the office. With no experience at all, he was being offered the plum part of Billy the pageboy in a new production of "Sherlock Holmes". The famous actor H.A. Saintsbury was playing the lead role. There was a chance, too, of another part in Saintsbury's own play, "Jim, a Romance of Cockayne", which was to run until the "Holmes" production was ready.

Charlie was sent to the very grand and dignified Green Room Club to meet the actor. His life had made him very shy – something people often took for stand-offishness – but Saintsbury liked him and set him at ease. Charlie emerged with both parts.

Rehearsals were unlike anything he had met before, for he had never acted, but Saintsbury was patient and Charlie quick to learn. He could scarcely read, but Sydney read his lines over to him and in three days, he was word perfect.

"Jim" was a dismal failure. It could have been very disheartening, but the critics found "one redeeming feature" in the show – Charlie Chaplin.

One wrote, "I have never seen the boy before, but I hope to hear great things of him in the future."

"Sherlock Holmes" opened on July 27, 1903 at the enormous "Pavilion Theatre" and after a short run went out on tour.

Charlie seemed to change overnight. It was as if he had found the thing he was meant to do. Dear, kind, capable Sydney was to become famous on

As a bellboy in "Sherlock Holmes" Charlie Chaplin was already, at the age of fourteen, making his mark as an actor. Although not all his appearances were great successes the ability was there and the audiences recognized it from the start.

the stage, too, but for him it was a job, just part of his life. For Charlie, his work was to be his world. Everything else fitted in around its edges.

He persuaded the management to give Sydney a small part. Hannah's state of mind improved and for a little while the three of them toured together, Hannah delighting in her boys' success.

The third tour of "Holmes" was a miserable business, for there had been a change of management. Charlie was saved by a telegram. He was offered a part in a play with William Gillette, a great American actor. It failed – but Gillette liked Charlie's work so much he gave him the part of Billy in his new production of "Sherlock Holmes".

It meant London's West End – and Charlie was still only sixteen.

Success and failure

Charlie learned a lot from Gillette. He was a fine actor and a patient teacher. He believed that stage drama developed from watching real life – something that Hannah and Charlie understood very well.

But for Hannah, there was no moving forward. The insanity she had fought for so long had returned, more violently than ever. Her sons were away and friends took her to the asylum. This time there was to be no recovery. In her lucid moments, she wrote her boys brave letters, trying hard to be cheerful and sending them her love.

Sydney was now appearing in a knock-about farce called "Repairs" – a sketch that involved a lot of water, ladders, buckets, paste, paper and falling about. At the end of "Sherlock Holmes" Charlie joined him.

Things seemed to be moving very fast, as though Charlie was eager to get somewhere just over the horizon. For a while, he was with a very popular act called the "Casey's Court Circus". The audiences loved him, especially when he raced about the stage, flinging one leg out for balance as he skidded around corners.

But success can be followed by disaster. Charlie, incredibly, set himself up as a Jewish entertainer.

Charlie Chaplin, at the age of sixteen, imitating a well-known "quack" doctor. Chaplin's great skill as a mime artist and impersonator were visible even at the beginning of his career. The tilt of the head, the look in the eye and the position of the fingers were absolutely perfect, and he took great detailed care over make-up and costume.

Five of Fred Karno's companies set off on tour from south London with Chaplin as one of their leading stars. Crowds of people gathered to see the actors off on their way to America or Europe. The companies and their stars, like today's most famous TV and pop personalities, were mobbed wherever they went.

He was so bad that he was booed from the stage. He had seen it happen to his mother, but it was a new experience for him. He stood in the wings, shaking – and he was never to feel happy with a live audience again.

Lucky break

This time it was Sydney's turn to rescue him. He was now a rising star in the successful Fred Karno's "Silent Comedians" and he persuaded his boss to give Charlie a two-week unpaid trial.

He was given a supporting part – but it was his big chance and he knew it. He made the most of every single thing he was asked to do, adding small unexpected tricks – and topping the stars' best lines.

to the audiences' huge delight. It did not endear him to the other performers, but Karno recognized talent, and Charlie was taken into the show.

He puzzled the rest of the company, he seemed so changeable. But a colleague, Stan Laurel – one day to join up with Oliver Hardy to make one of the greatest comedy duos of all time – liked him. He saw that Charlie was both shy and utterly absorbed in his work. He knew that he could be as much fun, and as kind and generous as the other actors – but that his work came first.

It was, by now, 1908, Charlie was nineteen – and he fell in love. Hetty Kelly was only fifteen and her parents quoshed the romance before it had really begun – but the memory of pretty Hetty stayed with Charlie all his life.

Touring with Fred Karno

Fred Karno was coarse, ignorant, even cruel, but he understood comedy. He taught Charlie that a touch of sentiment can add to a humorous situation, a fact Charlie was to employ over and over again in his films.

In 1910, when Karno set off on his yearly American tour, Charlie was included in the group. He was a tremendous hit with the Americans.

"One of the best pantomime artists ever seen here." They were away for twenty-one months and Charlie came home to find Sydney married. The next American tour began five months later, but Charlie found himself more and more dissatisfied with the way it was being organized. Nevertheless, the tour was a great success – and so was Charlie.

They had reached Philadelphia when a telegram arrived.

"Is there a man named Chaffin in your company or something like that – if so will he communicate with Kessel and Baumann...."

Charlie, intrigued, took a day to go to see these mysterious gentlemen in New York. To his astonishment, he found that they had seen his act and that he was being offered the chance to replace a star in the Keystone film company.

It was May 1913 – and Charlie's whole life was about to change.

"For years I have specialized in one type of comedy – strictly pantomime. I have measured it, gauged it, studied. I have been able to establish exact principles to govern its reactions on audiences. It has a certain pace and tempo. Dialogue, to my way of thinking, always slows action, because action must wait upon words."

Charlie Chaplin.

Charlie discovers film

Cinema – the kinematograph – was born in the same year as Charlie. At first, audiences were dumbfounded to see moving pictures – incidents that lasted only a few moments – but by 1913 cinema was becoming big business. Keystone was one of the companies churning out short films to meet the demand; though people still believed it was a passing fad, and would never replace live shows.

Studios were not like the elaborate places they are today. In his biography, *Chaplin. His Life and Art*, David Robinson desribes the one for which Charlie was heading: "An area of 150 feet square was surrounded by a green board fence. At the

Above left: Dated about 1890, this machine showed moving pictures of the kind of entertainment to be seen on the stage – jugglers and mime artists.

Above: A camera from 1889 with sixteen lenses which each took separate pictures on a photographic plate.

Left: When rotated at a particular speed, this disk showed the horse and rider racing along. It is one of the early inventions that led to the cinema equipment used today.

centre stood the stage, overhung with white linen to diffuse the sunlight. An old bungalow housed the offices and the women's dressing rooms; some converted agricultural buildings served as dressing rooms for the men."

That was it.

There was no sound, but in romantic films a small orchestra was sometimes hired to get the actors into the right mood. The handcranked cameras were in fixed positions. The actor obeyed the camera rather than the other way around.

Much of the footage was shot in a garden or in the streets outside the studio. At first, everything depended on the sun, for there were no studio lights.

Keystone

Charlie had been very excited by Keystone's offer, but now that he was actually in Hollywood, he wondered if he had done the right thing. After all, he was a stage comedian. For several days, he was too nervous even to go down to the studio. It took an urgent 'phone call from Sennett, his new boss, to get him there.

He was completely unnerved by what he saw. His comedy had always depended on rehearsal, on careful timing and clever, calculated effect. Keystone did not believe in such subtleties.

The Keystone comedies relied on slapstick, headlong chases and grotesque make-up. But Charlie was not going to be beaten. He was kept hanging about for several weeks and he used the time to watch and to learn. He was determined to master this new medium. It offered him the chance of money and success – and it would set him free from the unpredictability of live audiences.

"He [Chaplin] was a strange, morbid, romantic creature, seemingly totally unconscious of the greatness that was in him."
Constance Collier.

Charlie's first film

Charlie's first film, released in February 1914, was a one-reeler that ran for about a quarter of an hour. It was called *Making a Living*. Even though he still knew very little about film, he understood comedy and he realized at once that the director was a

complete incompetent. He was bitterly disappointed in the finished piece. Everything that he had suggested had been cut from the final footage.

Nevertheless, the public liked it – and spotted Charlie, in a frockcoat and top hat, as "a comedian of the first water".

Dissatisfaction only made Charles Spencer Chaplin determined to do better in future.

Sennett had one sure way of saving money on sets and extras. He took his crew to some local event and let his actors loose among the crowd.

Charlie's second film was made at a children's car race. He was told to fit himself out with a costume and then make a nuisance of himself at the track.

Many of Charlie Chaplin's films dealt with serious issues – but in their own comical way. Chaplin made falling over, throwing pies and street chases look easy and spontaneous; each shot was painstakingly worked out to get it just right, no matter how many times he had to fall over in order to get the exact effect he wanted.

The Little Tramp is born

He chose a bowler hat, slightly too small for him, a tight jacket, outsize pants, enormous boots and a jaunty little swagger cane – the Little Tramp made his very first appearance on the screen. Even Charlie could never have guessed how famous and enduring this character was to become. But right from the very first moment, he knew just how The Tramp would behave – a man down on his luck, but bravely attempting some sort of dignity.

He remembered the impoverished clerks of his childhood, who chalked their collars, inked the bare patches on their sleeves and trimmed the frayed edges of their shirts to look respectable. He remembered the way even the most desperately poor men, women and children always wore a hat, however dilapidated.

Long after, he was to tell an interviewer that he had picked up the toes-out shuffle watching an old drunk when he was a child. In all his films he was to draw on that storehouse of memories.

The Tramp had shown himself, but there were to be many more films before he took on his final character. For the time being, Charlie played all sorts of characters. He was good, but he was still just one comedian among many others. In these early films there are brief glimpses of the charm and imagination of his later work, but they are usually fast, crude and sometimes brutal, relying on kicks and punches and falls for laughs.

Experience

Charlie's first two-reeler, *Mabel at the Wheel*, was made in April 1914. Since February, he had made ten films and he had learned a lot – but he was far from happy. He now knew what was possible in film, yet all his suggestions were being ignored. When Charlie knew for sure that he was right, he would stand up to anyone, and he tackled Mack Sennett, demanding better treatment.

Sennett was important and nearly sacked him – but the public loved him and the distributors were demanding more and more Chaplin films.

Opposite: A smart and sophisticated Chaplin. Without his costume it is difficult to recognize that woebegone little Tramp or to see the street urchin that he had been as a child.

Below: This is a film still or single shot from 1915. Chaplin is seen here without his famous little moustache and the camera on the right is taking pictures of the actors. When he was with Keystone Chaplin developed his own distinctive style of acting and eventually directed almost all the films he appeared in.

Sennett was forced to give in to Charlie's demand and from then until he left the Keystone studio, Chaplin directed all the films in which he appeared, with one exception.

In an incredibly short time, Charlie Chaplin had done what he had set out to do. He had become a very important man in motion pictures ... but he was paying the price.

When he had first arrived at Keystone, he joined the others for a drink after work or went to a boxing match with them: but as the pressure of work grew, so his social life faded. It was Karno all over again. Work was for Charlie more important than anything else. He was often very lonely.

"Business is business"

Chaplin's contract with Sennett was coming to an end. He wrote to Syd, elated and astounded by his sudden rise to fame:

"The whole of my time is taken up with the

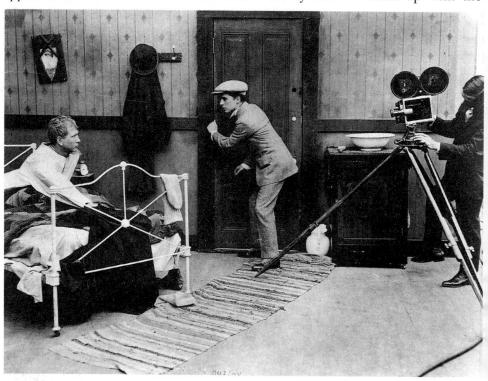

movies. I write, direct and play in them and believe me it keeps you busy. Well, Sid, I have made good. All the theatres feature my name in big letters, i.e. 'Chas Chaplin hear [sic] today.' I tell you in this country I am a box office attraction. All the managers tell me that I have fifty letters a week from men and women in all parts of the world. It is wonderfull [sic] how popular I am in such a short time and next year I hope to make a bunch of dough."

Lack of education had not held Charlie back ... and he was a shrewd businessman. He knew he must move on. "Mr. Sennett is a lovely man and we are pals, but business is business."

It was a risk, but one that had to be taken. After some disappointments and anxieties, he eventually signed with the Essanay Film Manufacturing Company of Chicago. In December 1914, Charlie left for Chicago, his apprentice days in film behind him.

Essanay

Chicago was cold and when Charlie saw Essanay's production methods, his heart grew even colder.

Keystone had been maddening at times, but at least it was alive and inventive. Essanay was simply a film sausage machine, and a badly-organized one at that, waste and scrimping going on side by side.

There were, however, some fine comedians there and Charlie made the best of what looked like a bad bargain.

His fellow workers were puzzled by him. He was already a great star and yet he lived simply and with very few possessions. His work, as always, was his life. He regarded it not as glamorous or exciting, but as a job to be done as perfectly as possible.

The studio had a bargain when they signed Chaplin to make fourteen films. *His New Job* was shot in only two weeks and made more money in advance sales than any previous Essanay picture.

But the cold of Chicago was too much for Charlie: he transferred to the studios in California – small, depressing, but warm.

Despite everything, Charlie made some good

films. Comedy changes. The audiences of 1915 roared with laughter at things today's audiences would probably find repetitive and heavy-handed. But the subtleties of Charlie's mime, the flash of his smile and his wonderful timing are all as fresh now as the day the camera captured them.

The Little Tramp

The Tramp was a big step forward. In it, the Little Tramp, whom most people remember when they think of Charlie Chaplin, put in his first proper appearance. The whole world was to take the character to its heart – small and shabby, a strange mixture of child and man, gentle, wistful, mischievous, brave – and always a survivor. Somehow, Charlie had found a character with whom everyone on earth could identify. His sadness and his type of comedy crossed every boundary. Being silent, everyone could understand him.

Charlie very much wanted to make a long picture, to be called *Life,* in which he intended to bring a greater realism and truth to his comedy. The Little Tramp would move through a world of loneliness and poverty such as that Charlie had known when he was young.

But the studio thought the film would not make money and Chaplin had to abandon the project. Essanay, however, took some of the footage and grafted it on to other films. Charlie was deeply hurt and angry, for it was now all out of context.

He always wanted experimental footage to be destroyed – for he did not want the public to be disillusioned. He remembered the sweating ballerinas and the sad, neurotic comedians of his youth – and he wanted his audiences only to see the final magic.

"*Some people consider movies the 20th century's greatest art form, and many consider Chaplin the movies' pre-eminent genius.*"

Leonard Maltin, from the article, "Silent-film buffs stalk and find a missing Tramp".

Genius

Fortunately, he was disobeyed. After his death, two British researchers, Kevin Brownlow and David Gill, tracked down incredible quantities of his discarded film and made it into a documentary that shows us how Charlie Chaplin created his films.

Only a genius could have discarded some of those
sequences. However long it had taken to shoot
them, if they didn't satisfy Chaplin, they were cut.
He pared his films to the bone.

In 1936, he was to tell the great French film-
maker, Jean Cocteau, that a film was like a tree.
When shaken, all that was loose and unnecessary

fell away, leaving only the essential form. When every inch of superfluous material had been discarded, the film was complete.

Essanay continued to anger Charlie to the last. He made a compact, two-reel skit on *Carmen*. The studio patched out-taken footage from other films into it and stretched it to a full length feature. The sprawling mess that resulted so horrified Chaplin that he became ill and had to go to bed for two days.

Fame

Charlie Chaplin was now famous – and he suffered for it. Many films were made by rival companies, quite blatantly using Chaplin look-alikes. Even his brother Sydney appeared as a rather tubby Tramp.

Charlie Chaplin madness seemed to have swept the world. The Little Tramp appeared in comic strips, film cartoons, as dolls, in books, in songs. In France they danced the Charlot One-Step.

Charlie himself was among the last to realize what was happening – he was far too busy.

No film actor had ever been so famous or so loved.

In February 1916, Charlie went to New York – and was stunned by his reception all along the route. The Chief of the New York police was forced to ask him to leave the train at the station before Grand Central, the waiting crowds were so vast.

Charlie was so famous now that every film studio was desperate for him to come and work for them. Sydney was acting as his manager and was

"The Dance of the Rolls" ... the sheer genius of Chaplin's work is captured in this sequence of six shots. Taken from "The Gold Rush", Chaplin is using two forks and bread rolls pretending that they are his feet and that he is dancing. They kick to the left and to the right and Charlie's face holds exactly the expression of the dancer. It is perfectly magical to watch and is a piece of Chaplin at his best.

determined to get the best deal possible. In the end, Charlie signed with Mutual for a staggering sum – the greatest in the history of the cinema until then. He was twenty-seven.

In pursuit of perfection

Charlie Chaplin set to work to build a little company of actors. He knew his capabilities now and his position meant that he could make movies as he wanted – spending more time on each one, and using more film. He was to become more ruthless than ever in his pursuit of perfection.

Today films cost so much to make they have to be made to a strict shooting schedule, but Charlie's grew like living things.

He would start with an idea, film it, change it, film it again, change the characters, change the set – and then discard everything he had shot and start again. He often went to the studio without any idea at all and just started filming.

He needed actors who would allow him to play every part through them. It was as if he wanted to project himself into their heads. He was incredibly versatile. He could play the cello and the violin; he was a gymnast, a dancer and a skater.

Above all, he could mime.

For example, there is a memorable sequence in *The Pawnshop* of 1916, in which pawnbroker Charlie assesses the value of a clock. He listens clinically to its workings with a stethoscope, then attacks it with a hammer and drill. After that, he

The Tramp, the eternal loser, looks so pitiful here that the audience cannot help but take him into their hearts. But the films always end with the Tramp getting the girl or winning the money. Many of Chaplin's films revolve around his personal hurt and anger against the persecution of people who were not thought to be "important". It is often this quality that makes his films endure.

opens it up with a can-opener, sniffs the contents and examines them meticulously with a watchmaker's glass. Dissatisfied, he pulls out the entire works with a pair of pliers and, as the mainspring runs amok, oils them.

His analysis complete, he sweeps the ruin into the customer's hat – and hands it back with a shrug. It is not worth pawning.

"The Immigrant"

By now he was a master of his craft. While some artists – writers, painters, film-makers – think everything out before they begin and then put it all down with scarcely any alteration being needed – actors, like Charlie, have to produce great quantities of work, and then cut it to shape.

The film, *The Immigrant*, released in June 1917, entailed *forty thousand feet* of film being shot. It took Charlie, helped by assistants, four days and four nights to cut it to the required *eighteen hundred feet*. He viewed each scene perhaps fifty times before he decided exactly where to cut. In the end Charlie was "dirty, haggard and collarless, but his film was finished". "The Immigrant" was the first in a series of Chaplin's great films that took up the serious social issues of his time. From 1917 until World War II his greatest films focussed on injustice – and many of them had a deep emotional effect on the people who saw them.

The Immigrant plays upon the plight of the poor entering America. In many ways it can be seen to be autobiographical – Charlie had come to the United States as a stranger and discovered both the good and the bad that the country had to offer.

In this film the Tramp is seen on board ship with a bizarre mixture of immigrants. The Tramp meets Edna and her mother who are penniless after being robbed by a gambler – and the story is a comic love story set against the terrible sufferings many immigrants had to endure. They were lured by stories of a golden land of opportunity, only to be met with rejection in the new land. In the film, the Statue of Liberty is seen in the background with the title "Arrival in the Land of Liberty"; but the crowds on board are immediately roped together like cattle by the immigration authorities.

> *"His [Chaplin's] audience in America consisted for the most part of large numbers of European immigrants and their descendants. Everyday life was often joyless: ordinary people had to contend with unemployment, corruption, a strict government and an elitist upper class. In the little tramp they saw in the cinema, they had an ally and a friend. When they saw waiters, barbers, students or policemen on the screen, it was the day-to-day reality they were used to, and the effect was a comic one."*
>
> Thomas Leeflang, from "The World of Comedy".

The eternal loser

Charlie, as the Tramp, is the eternal loser who always wins in the end. He bridges the gap between rich and poor, the successful and the losers – he stands as the little man who triumphs in the face of all difficulties. Charlie gives some dignity to the less fortunate, giving them a chance to laugh at themselves, knowing that they can always win in the end. It is this quality that gives the Tramp universal popularity – he breaks down all social barriers in his audience.

World War I

In 1914, World War I had broken out and some people felt that Charlie should have returned to Britain to fight for his country – he was not an

American citizen. But others felt that Charlie Chaplin's films were doing more good – bringing laughter and hope into those dark days as well as making a lot of money for America – than one small soldier could ever have done.

Chaplin contributed to the war in the best way he knew how – he made a film. In May 1918, Charlie – by now with First National – began the film, *Shoulder Arms*. The war was four years old and Charlie made what seemed an astonishing decision. He would make a comedy set *in the trenches*.

Until this time, most films had been a series of separate incidents strung together. Now they were beginning to be properly constructed, like stage plays ... and they were no longer regarded as entertainment only for the masses.

Shoulder Arms was so clear in Chaplin's mind that he filmed, very rapidly, scene after scene of wonderful comedy. (It was to be sixty-five years before that footage was seen, when the out-takes were found and included in a television documentary, *The Unknown Chaplin*.) After a month, Charlie discarded everything that he had shot, built new sets, and began again.

In the film, Charlie took the terrible reality known to every serving soldier – the endless mud of Flanders, the water-logged trenches, the lice and rats, the constant bombardment and the fear – and transformed it all into a comedy that mocked the idiocy of war.

Shoulder Arms was released in October 1918, a month before the armistice was signed marking the end of World War I. The returning troops loved it. They called themselves "Fred Karno's Army". Being able to laugh at the insanity of war had been their only real defence.

Marriage

Two days after its release, Charlie married Mildred Harris, pretty in the same child-like way as his first love, Hetty Kelly.

He was famous, good-looking and very, very rich – and he fell in love only too easily. This made him

Mildred Harris and Charlie Chaplin were married in October 1918. Mildred was the first of his four wives and it was not a happy marriage. In his early marriages Chaplin seemed to be searching for his childhood sweetheart, Hetty Kelly, and failing to find what he was looking for.

the target for pretty girls, greedy for a part in a movie and a share in his fortune.

The trouble was, Charlie Chaplin's whole mind and heart were dominated by his work. In consequence, he fell out of love almost as fast as he fell into it.

The marriage to Mildred was hopeless from the very start. Charlie was so unhappy that even film-making became a nightmare. However, he made an important decision. He began to plan an independent studio, in partnership with the man he regarded as his only real friend, Douglas Fairbanks, Fairbanks' wife, Mary Pickford, and film director D.W. Griffith. It was to be called United Artists.

By now, Charlie and Mildred were expecting their first baby any day. If Charlie had hoped the new baby would save the failing marriage, he was tragically wrong. On July 7, 1919 Mildred gave birth to a boy, Norman Spencer – but the baby only lived for three days. Charlie was heartbroken.

"The Kid"

He had only one way to face such sorrow. He threw himself into work on a new feature-length film called *The Kid*.

At least Charlie had the perfect actor for the title role – four-year-old Jackie Coogan. Chaplin was at a stage show watching Jackie's father, an eccentric dancer. He'd brought his son on stage at the end of his act. Jackie imitated his father with gusto and brought the house down – just as the young Charlie had once done. Chaplin met the family at their hotel and he and Jackie, the little boy, took to each other at once. Chaplin coaxed a wonderful performance from Jackie. The tale of the Tramp and the Kid touched everyone's hearts and the film was a great success, eventually being shown in fifty countries.

The Kid tackled another social concern that deeply upset Charlie Chaplin – the treatment of abandoned children. He had *never* forgotten the fear he had felt when he had been taken in to an orphanage. The opening scene shows Edna "Whose

Baggy pants, tight coat, bowler hat, large shoes and the small moustache were Charlie's trademark. By 1916 he was the most famous actor in the United States. He was also adored across the world. The poor little Tramp was fast becoming one of the world's richest men.

Jackie Coogan as "The Kid" and Charlie Chaplin as the Tramp made a memorable team. The film is far more than a sad and funny tale – it tells of the love and bonding between a child and its "parent". In a fierce statement against the orphanages that he experienced in his own childhood, Chaplin shows the absolute importance for a child to be part of a family – however small or inadequate. The two should not be parted.

only sin was motherhood" leaving hospital with her baby. Thinking about committing suicide she leaves the baby in the back of an expensive car with a note attached, asking the finder to protect and care for him. The car is stolen and the baby dumped in an alley where the Tramp finds him and, unwillingly, becomes his guardian. The Tramp then has to learn how to look after the baby: making a cradle from a hammock and a bottle from an old coffee-pot.

Jackie Coogan appears as the child at five years old. The friendship between Charlie and Jackie comes through on the screen and adds to the poignant, loving relationship the two have forged. The Kid and the Tramp go into business, getting out of scrapes with the law in touching, humorous ways.

But the Kid's mother has not forgotten her child and is now a successful opera singer; she comes across the Kid and the Tramp mid-brawl but does not recognize him. It is not until the Kid falls ill and the Tramp, after trying to cure the child himself, calls a doctor that Edna finds out the boy is hers. When the doctor asks Charlie if he is the boy's father, he shows the note that he found attached to the baby – the orphan authorities are notified so that the boy can receive "Proper care and attention". At the same time Edna has been told that the Kid fits the description of her missing child.

David Robinson, in his biography of Chaplin, describes the following scene as "the most extraordinary in the film, and indeed one of the most memorable in the whole history of cinema". The Kid is bundled like a stray into the orphanage wagon. The distressed Tramp, followed by a policeman, leaps over the rooftops to stop the van and rescue his "son". As he saves the Kid from the perils of the orphanage the Tramp becomes a hero.

The film ends with the Kid reunited with his mother and the Tramp being invited in to the magnificent mansion.

"The Kid" was a success in a different way to Charlie Chaplin's other films; there is more drama and very little comedy. The audiences loved it for its strong emotional appeal. The abandoned child needed love, and the Tramp, poor and unqualified as a parent, was the only person who could provide that. The love that developed between "father" and "son" was so strong it could not be broken.

Divorce

But Charlie's private world continued to fall apart. In April, 1920, Mildred began divorce proceedings and in November they were officially divorced.

At last, life seemed more tranquil and in 1921,

Chaplin became frustrated with film companies and their directors and took complete control over all his work. He directed and edited his films, shooting thousands of feet of film and then discarding everything – only to begin again. Here he inspects the rushes or first stages of "The Kid", a film that became a classic. So, to his great skills as mimic and business man was added that of brilliant film editor.

Charlie sent friends to fetch Hannah, his mother, to the United States. To her delight, they fitted her out with a whole wardrobe of new clothes.

Her mind was still confused, but she enjoyed the voyage and, apart from mistaking a customs officer for Jesus Christ, behaved normally. After all the years of poverty and sorrow and those spent in a home for the mentally disturbed, she was, at last, settled into a home of her own. She was not in the least put out by the change and although she was inclined to offer ice-cream to every passer-by, she was calm and contented. Ice-cream had always been a sign of good times in her family!

Old scenes, new horizons

On August 22, 1921, Charlie suddenly abandoned the new film he was working on and announced that he was going to Europe. Five days later, he sailed for London.

The past and the present swirled together in his mind. In 1910 he had sailed to America with Fred Karno, a young comedian grateful for a job. Now, only eleven years later, he was perhaps one of the most famous men in the world.

At every station on the railway journey to London, people were waiting to see his train pass and London was packed with cheering crowds.

He slipped away from the hotel where he was staying, by a back entrance, and revisited the places that he had known in the hungry, anxious years of his childhood and which he had recreated in many of his films. It seemed another world, another Charlie, that he was remembering – yet so many things had scarcely changed at all. He was, after all, only thirty-two.

He met people he had known in that other exist ence, but it was no longer his world, even if he had kept his respect for those struggling against poverty and his pity for those who had been overcome by it. He was meeting other people now – famous people, writers and actors and politicians. And on equal terms. On impulse, he moved on to France and to Germany, but in October 1921 he was on his way back to the United States.

"The Gold Rush"

Once in Los Angeles, he got down to completing the last films of the First National contract. The studio had caused him a lot of trouble – at one point he had thought of suing them for ten million dollars – and he wanted to be free of them.

When he had finished *The Pilgrim* Charlie was able to begin making films for United Artists. The new picture was his seventy-second. He only had a tiny part in it, which confused his public, but in his next film he gave them back the Tramp, and more imaginatively than ever.

Once again, he chose the most unlikely of subjects for his inspiration, and once again he dedicated his comic genius to tackling a great social

In "The Gold Rush" Chaplin eats his boot. In a comic mastery of the mannerisms of people eating a special treat, it really appears that he is enjoying his meal. (The boot was actually made of liquorice!) The realism Chaplin achieves with facial expressions and the way he chews each mouthful is another glimpse of the brilliance of his miming ability.

injustice. He had been reading about the sufferings of the gold prospectors in the Klondike – and he decided to make *The Gold Rush,* which was to be one of his most famous films.

It was packed with comic inventions, but there were moments of pathos, too. Poor Charlie goes to infinite trouble to prepare a dinner party for the girl he loves and her friends. No one comes. In the end, Charlie wins the girl's love *and* finds gold.

There were none of the electronic visual effects of today. Everything had to be achieved by building elaborate models, by inventing clever mechanisms, by calculating camera shots – and by cutting.

The studio "mountains" and "blizzard" needed 239,577 feet of timber, 22,750 feet of plaster, 285 tons of salt, 100 barrels of flour and 4 cartloads of confetti. Charlie had shot even more film than usual: he edited it from 231,505 feet to 8,555 feet!

But, if on screen Chaplin's story had ended happily, in real life things were far different.

In November, 1924, Charlie had married his leading lady, Lita Grey. It was no wiser a marriage than his first had been. Two sons, Sydney and Charles, were born – but the marriage went from bad to worse and in 1926, Lita took the children and left home. Charlie emerged from it very well, but it was another black period in his life.

Perfection

Despite the turmoil in his private life, Charlie went on and made a film called *The Circus.* Things were made even harder when in September 1927 a fire swept through the studio, completely destroying the set. But he simply carried on.

It took him just a week to learn to walk the tightrope. The sigh of relief when it was all over soon turned to a sigh of exasperation. Bad laboratory work had ruined all the "wire" takes – and he had to do the whole thing again. In the end, Chaplin had done over seven hundred takes on that tightrope – and all for a few minutes of film.

Perhaps his time in the lions' cage was even more frightening. It took two hundred takes to complete

Chaplin went back home to London in 1921. The crowds mobbed him outside the Ritz Hotel – not far from the shabby streets of his childhood.

that sequence – and Charlie was to say later that the terror on his face in the film was not acting!

The divorce from Lita and a federal tax demand meant that Charlie was in urgent need of money. The moment *The Circus* was completed, he launched into making *City Lights*.

But there was to be another blow. On August 28, 1928, his mother died. Hannah had been very ill, but she and Charlie had been laughing together the day before. That night she fell into a coma and only roused once before her death.

Watching her suffering had been almost too much for him. Now he stood by her bed and saw that death had taken away all her confusion and pain. He remembered the songs and the stories and the ice-cream summer, and he wept.

Internationally popular, Chaplin films and publicity posters were translated into many languages.

Opposite: This poster advertizes the film "City Lights". Stylized posters of Chaplin appeared everywhere, along with hundreds of toys and "Tramp" impersonators. He was immensely popular. Everybody wanted a part of the Chaplin success story.

In the early films the Tramp would walk off into the distance for the final scene – perhaps indicating better things to come in the future, and a touch of sadness at seeing him go. For the first time, in "Modern Times", the Tramp is not alone.

He said of Hannah, "If it had not been for my mother I doubt if I could have made a success of pantomime. She was one of the greatest pantomime artists I have ever seen."

In the next few years Charlie was to make three of his finest films: *City Lights* in 1931, *Modern Times* in 1936 and *The Great Dictator* in 1940.

Sound had arrived, but Charlie distrusted it. He believed that the language of mime could cross frontiers as the spoken word never could. Even though Warner Brothers released *The Lights of New York,* the first all-talking picture, just as Charlie started work on *City Lights,* he stuck to silence.

City Lights was perhaps the greatest of all his later films, but it took two years of work and worry to make. In the story the Tramp saves the money to cure a blind flower-seller – who imagines he is a millionaire. Once she can see, the Tramp is too nervous to tell her who had given the money.... Charlie wanted perfection and he shot tiny scenes over and over again. But when it was complete, none of the struggle showed. It was a well-balanced film, full of comedy and tenderness. He had shot 314,256 feet of film to achieve the 8,093 feet that was run. What remained was a masterpiece.

The London première was in February 1931 – and Charlie went to England to attend it.

Old times

This time he visited his old school at Hanwell, and was overwhelmed by memories. This visit seemed to bring his past more vividly to life and to drive away all the old nightmares.

Charlie had few fond memories of the country of his birth and annoyed many people by his outspokenness on "patriotism". He had seen for himself what patriotism could lead to – blind ignorance and bigotry.

"Patriotism is the greatest insanity the world has ever suffered. I have been all over Europe in the past few months. Patriotism is rampant everywhere and the result is going to be another war." He was right ... though it lay eight years in the future.

Above: In "Modern Times" Chaplin was commenting on the monotony and boredom of modern factory work. As in most of his films he made an important point about society but in a purely comical way.

He went on to the Far East, where he was greeted as warmly as in Europe. Charlie's silence needed no translation. The Little Tramp was a universal friend.

Back to Hollywood

Charlie arrived back in Hollywood in June 1932. He was now forty-three and very distressed by all the hardship and misery he had met on his travels. He tried to work out a system of economics that would solve the universal problems of unemployment, poverty and injustice. He did not know enough to understand the complexity of the difficulties and his system could never have worked.

But what he *could* do was make a film.

And so his next film was *Modern Times*. It shows the Tramp caught up in a world where money means more than people, who are treated like cogs in a huge machine. In the end, he escapes with the waif he has befriended.

As always, the film was based in comedy and was Chaplin's reaction to five million unemployed in the United States. In earlier films the Tramp was poor, but in *Modern Times* he was one of the millions of ordinary people coping with strikes, factory conditions, low pay or unemployment.

A few years later, *Modern Times* was seen as proof that Charlie was a communist.

Charlie fell in love with the girl playing the waif, Paulette Goddard, and they were married.

He was a difficult man to live with, easily irritated and annoyed by petty things. Paulette was an intelligent and gifted girl and she must have found it hard to put up with. Quietly, she built a career in films for herself – and in 1942, after seven years, Chaplin's third marriage was to come to an end.

World War II

But now it was 1938. Charlie had been right. War was coming. In Germany, the Nazi party, led by Adolf Hitler, had gained control. Minority groups, especially Jews, were being murdered in a plan to "purify the race". At gigantic rallies, Hitler was whipping the German people up into a frenzy of patriotism and ambition.

Strangely, not many people outside Germany realized what was happening. Many saw Hitler not as a dangerous fanatic, but a strutting clown. Charlie himself watched events in Germany and Spain and grew more and more disturbed.

In October 1938, he began work on a film called *The Great Dictator* in which he attempted to warn the world about the danger of Hitler's magnetic popularity. He mocked Hitler by acting both the dictator, "Heinkel" and a Jewish tailor who is his double. The days of improvization and silence were over. There was a proper script – and sound.

The film was full of wonderful comedy, but Charlie felt he had to speak out. The little tailor, who has changed places with Heinkel, makes a long speech in which he implores the armies to come to their senses.

"The Great Dictator" was a topical film, started in 1938, in an attempt to warn people of the danger of Adolf Hitler's beliefs. It made its statement at a time when the world was in turmoil. As usual Chaplin used comedy for a deeply serious subject but for once he grew to regret the technique. He said later that he could not have made the film had he known about the concentration camps that Hitler had set up to kill millions of Jewish people.

Above and opposite: The international posters and promotions continued even as Chaplin went through a distressing court case. Chaplin's films seemed to stand on their own despite the personal troubles of their creator.

"Let us fight for a world of reason, a world where science and progress will lead to all men's happiness. Soldiers in the name of democracy, let us unite."

It was a hopeless gesture. By the time the film was released in 1940, all Europe was at war and the whole world realized what had been happening.

Persecution

So far, the United States had not been drawn into the European conflict, but on December 7, 1941, the Japanese attacked Pearl Harbor and the United States was forced into the war.

Charlie Chaplin was disturbed by the fact that America, the country he loved so much, seemed neither to know nor to care about the suffering of the Russian allies, who were standing against the ferocious attacks of the German invaders with such incredible courage.

He did not trust the Russian leader, Stalin, but Chaplin deeply respected the Russian people and he spoke at many rallies, demanding "military help for Russia" – and unnerving his audiences by addressing them as "Comrades". He said: "I am not a Communist. I am a human being and I think I know the reactions of human beings. The Communists are no different from anyone else; when they lose an arm or a leg, they suffer as all of us do, and die as all of us die. And the Communist mother is the same as any other mother. When she receives the tragic news that her sons will not return, she weeps as other mothers weep."

The Russians lost twenty million people in the war. But words like this were to count against Chaplin in the years ahead.

Meanwhile, Charlie had troubles of his own. A mentally-disturbed woman named Joan Barry had broken into his house with a gun threatening to kill herself and now claimed he was the father of her baby. Although this was proved to be a lie, Charlie was dragged through the courts for three long years.

But this time, he did not face the ordeal alone. In 1942, he had met a young woman, the daughter

of the great American playwright, Eugene O'Neill.
She was only seventeen and a half, but she and
Charlie had fallen deeply in love.

Her name was Oona.

She had about her a quiet radiance, a gentleness
and a shyness that set her apart, but Charlie also
saw in her both intelligence and courage.

Oona's mother approved of their plan to marry,
but, perhaps understandably, her father was against
it. Charlie was, after all, fifty-four – and he had
been married three times. Charlie and Oona decided to put off the wedding until Oona was
eighteen and no longer needed her father's consent.

On June 16, 1943, Charlie and Oona were
married. Their first daughter, Geraldine, was born
on August 1, 1944.

In January 1945, Chaplin began work on
Monsieur Verdoux, a black comedy once more
based on a macabre reality, a mass-murderer
named Landru. The Little Tramp had gone – in
Verdoux, Charlie appears as a sophisticated
silver-haired gentleman, given to murder as a means
of income. It was a most bitter satire – for the arms

53

manufacturer in the story is a respected business-man, even if he is responsible for the death of thousands. Verdoux is executed. The arms manu-facturer continues in his trade.

The Barry case behind him, Charlie seemed to have found a time of peace and happiness; but America had become affected by a kind of madness, an obsessive fear and hatred of Communism.

A citizen of the world

Instead of reporters asking him about *Verdoux*, they were accusing Charlie of Communist sympathies. They paid no attention to his quiet and reasonable replies to their questions.

He gladly admitted that he had admired the cour-age of the Russians in the war and that he had liberal friends. He was proud of his friendships with men like the black actor, Paul Robeson, and the playwright Berthold Brecht, both of whom were Communists. Charlie had always been grateful to America for all it had done for him, but, first and

A massive fear of communism in the United States in the 1950s led to a "witch hunt" of communist sympathizers led by Senator McCarthy. Here a committee of McCarthy supporters sit in judgment on a citizen they suspect of being a communist. Chaplin, with his strong beliefs in humanity, was among the many individuals who was investigated in this way. He was eventually exiled and did not return to the United States for twenty years.

foremost, he considered himself to be a citizen of the world.

He spoke clearly, "I am not a communist. I am a peace-monger."

Intelligent people were disgusted and disturbed by this persecution and Charlie took heart from their support – but the Un-American Activities Committee was growing in power and hysteria. Anyone who had belonged to, or even sympathized with, the most faintly left wing organization was in danger of being branded a traitor to his country.

The Catholic War Veterans began to demand Chaplin's deportation. On one occasion, the FBI cross-examined Charlie for four hours. They questioned him about his personal life and his racial origins. Bravely he refused point blank to say that he hated all Communists.

Against this atmosphere of persecution, he set to work on a new film. He could not afford to let the studio stand idle.

The film was *Limelight*, the story of an aging music hall performer and the young girl he helps to success. Into it, he put his memories of the London and the theatrical life he had known as a boy. It was sentimental – but the knock-about comedy and the sentimentality of the old music hall ran through most of his films.

Sydney gave Charlie support, as did Oona. In 1946, their second child, Michael, was born and in 1949, Josephine. Victoria was born in 1951.

McCarthyism

America's anti-communist emotions had found a new and more lunatic voice. In 1950, a senator named Joseph McCarthy declared that he had a list of two hundred Communists in the State Department. On the new wave of hysteria, almost anyone could find themselves accused of anti-American activities and in court, being cross-examined and reviled by McCarthy and his cronies. Fear grew. Decent, intelligent, gifted people were losing their jobs and having their reputations destroyed. Lies were everywhere. People used McCarthy to settle

"I am an artist, not a politician."

Charlie Chaplin.

It was the close support and love of his fourth wife, Oona, that gave Charlie strength through these difficult times. Although many people disapproved of their marriage because of the thirty-six year age difference, it was to be the most permanent and perfect relationship in Charlie's life.

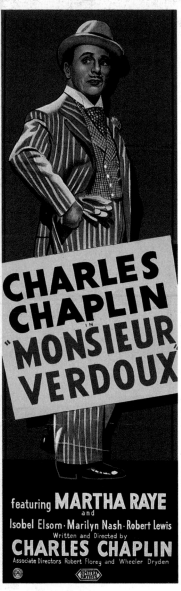

"*Monsieur Verdoux*" in which there was no sign of the little Tramp.

Opposite: An older Charlie Chaplin – still handsome and charming.

old scores – or saved their own skins by accusing innocent people.

Hollywood was especially vulnerable. A few brave men and women stood against the insanity – but many lost everything and were never to be employed in the film industry again.

Limelight completed, Charlie decided to take it to London for its première.

When the ship had been two days at sea, it was announced that the U.S. Attorney General had forbidden Chaplin re-entry to the United States.

He was an exile.

Love in exile

Charlie was received warmly in London and hailed as a genius. In the United States, the vicious attacks continued, but some newspapers kept their heads:

"Chaplin is an artist whose shining talent has for decades cast its lustre upon his adopted country and brought joy to the world," wrote *The Nation*.

But the FBI had been questioning the family's servants, trying to find material to blacken Charlie's name. They cross-examined Lita Grey, who had been his wife twenty-five years before, but she bravely refused to say anything that might harm him.

Charlie could not go back, and so the family left for Switzerland. In January 1953, they settled in the beautiful house at Corsier-sur-Vevey that was to be Charlie's home for the rest of his life.

If America had denounced Charlie, he had his family – by now, five children – Geraldine, Michael, Josephine, Victoria and Eugene – and the acclaim of the rest of the world.

Recognition

In May 1954, Charlie Chaplin was awarded the World Peace Council Prize. He gave the money to help the poor of Paris and London.

He began to make another film – *A King in New York* – but, sadly, it was not a success. It was an attack on McCarthyism, and perhaps his bitterness suffocated his genius.

The London première of
"A King in New York" –
the crowds break through
the police barriers and
almost besiege Chaplin.
Right: Putting make-up on
to play a fading comedian
in "Limelight". Chaplin
would say, "To work is to
live – and I love to live",
and he never did stop
working.

Three more children were born – Jane in 1957, Annette in 1959 and Christopher in 1962. The Chaplin family was complete.

In 1962 Charlie, who had never had a proper education, was granted honorary doctorates by Oxford and Durham universities.

But there was sorrow, too. On his birthday in 1965, Charlie heard that his brother Sydney had died.

In 1971, Paris awarded Charlie the prestigious "Grande Medaille de Vermeil" – and in 1972 America rediscovered him.

America forgives

McCarthy and his henchmen, who had destroyed the happiness of so many men and women, had been totally discredited in 1954, when it was discovered that they had been faking evidence.

Now America opened its arms to Charlie once more and he was showered with awards. Los Angeles, which had banned him from their "Walk of Fame", hastily added his name to it. He was given a rapturous welcome in New York and presented with the Handel Medallion. In Hollywood, to great acclaim, he was given a special Academy Award. The pageant of praise continued. In Venice, St. Mark's Square was turned into an open-air cinema to show *City Lights* and Charlie was awarded the Golden Lion of the Venice Film Festival.

Sir Charles Chaplin

In 1975, just before his eighty-sixth birthday, Charlie, who had been one of London's "infant poor" in the days of Queen Victoria, was knighted by Queen Elizabeth II. He was now Sir Charles Spencer Chaplin.

After a life of incredibly hard work, of great triumphs and great sorrows and trials, Charlie seemed to have entered a golden time. He was becoming frail, but loved to work as always.

"To work is to live – and I love to live," he said.

Charlie Chaplin talked of making another film, but was too old and weak. For a long while, Oona

Chaplin was given receptions and awards all over the world – especially in America. The great comedian who had done so much for cinema and for his audiences everywhere was once again welcomed into the country he had made his home and which had given him so much.

Above: The fluidity of movement, the dancing and the smile – even as an old man Chaplin had not lost any of his mastery. The audience was as captivated as they always had been.
Right: The Chaplin family. Oona and Charlie had eight children and were married for thirty-four happy years.

would not let anyone help her take care of him but in the end, she was persuaded to accept a nurse.

Christmas Eve, 1977 came and the house was brimming with children and grandchildren. "Father Christmas" arrived to distribute presents from the shining tree and when Charlie had been settled in his room, they left the door open so that he could share in the sounds of excitement and happiness that ran through the house.

In the morning, when it was time to wake him and to wish him a Happy Christmas, it was found that Charlie had died in his sleep. He was eighty eight years old.

It was a good day for someone who had given so much laughter and encouragement to the world to slip away.

Glossary

Apathy: Total disinterest in anything that is generally considered to be interesting or exciting.

Asylum: An institution providing shelter and support for blind, deaf and, especially, mentally-ill people.

Brewer's dray: The low cart which beer-makers used to transport beer.

Communist: A supporter of communism: the belief in the theory of common ownership of the means of production, distribution and supply by a classless society. Each person works according to ability and receives according to need. It is based on Karl Marx's belief that for there to be a more equal distribution of wealth, capitalism must be replaced by a working class government.

Dilapidated: Fallen into disrepair, in a state of ruin.

F.B.I.: The Federal Bureau of Investigation. The United States government agency with responsibility for investigating violations of federal law. It is particularly concerned with internal security.

"Five stones": A game played with five stones and a small ball. The object is to pick up the stones, while bouncing and catching the ball.

Footage: The amount of film material that has been shot or exposed.

Hansom cab: A two-wheeled carriage drawn by a horse with the driver sitting on the outside at the back.

Herring: A small fish with large silvery scales, from northern seas. When smoked, they are called "kippers".

Impersonation: The imitation of another person. The character and mannerisms, as well as clothes, are all carefully copied.

Indomitable: Difficult to subdue or defeat.

Infirmary: A place where the sick are cared for.

Klondike: A region in N.W. Canada in the basin of the Klondike River. It was rich in gold deposits in the late 1800s but was quickly exhausted by the many prospectors who went there.

Lucid: Usually this means clear or easily understood but it also refers to the periods of normality between the disturbed times that an insane person suffers.

Music hall: A place offering light entertainment consisting of short variety acts. Music halls were extremely popular in Britain in the early twentieth century.

Neurotic: A person who is emotionally unstable or suffers from the mental disorder, neurosis. This manifests itself in hysteria, anxiety or depression.

Outwork: Work that can be completed away from the factory, such as sewing on home sewing machines.

Pathos: The feeling of pity, sympathy or sorrow.

Pawnbroker: Someone who lends money in exchange for personal property left as security. If the money is not paid back within a given length of time the article can be sold.

Pedlars (U.S.: Peddlers): Street sellers who carried their wares about with them, they shouted out their prices to the passers-by.

Poignant: Distressing or painful to the feelings.

Property basket: The basket or container that holds all the movable objects and clothes used on the set of a play or film.

Ringworm: A type of fungal infection which usually shows itself as itchy circles on the skin.

Versatile: Able to adapt to a variety of different uses or skills.

Workhouse: A public institution in Britain where the poor were given food and lodging in return for work.

Peddlers: Street sellers who carried their wares about with them, they shouted out their prices to the passers-by.

Important Dates

1889 April 16: Charles Spencer Chaplin – Charlie Chaplin – is born in London.

1894 Charlie, aged five, gives his first stage performance.

1895 Charlie's mother, Hannah, enters Lambeth Infirmary.

1896 Charlie and his brother, Sydney, enter Hanwell Schools for the Infant Poor.

1898 Charlie, aged nine, leaves school.
Dec: Charlie joins the Eight Lancashire Lads.

1903 Hannah is admitted to Cane Hill asylum. She is readmitted several more times through her life.
July 6: Charlie plays Sam in "Jim, A Romance of Cockayne".
July 27: "Sherlock Holmes", with Charlie Chaplin aged fourteen, opens in London and then goes on tour.

1908 Charlie signs his first contract with Fred Karno.

1910 Charlie tours the U.S.A. for the first time.

1913 Charlie Chaplin, aged twenty-four, goes to work at Keystone in Hollywood.

1914 Feb: *Making a Living,* the first of the thirty-five films that Charlie makes with Keystone, is released.
June: World War I breaks out and Chaplin is criticized for not enlisting.
Dec: Charlie moves to Essanay. He makes fourteen films with this company.

1915 April: *The Tramp* is released.

1916 Charlie signs with the Mutual Film Corporation and ten films are released this year. He is twenty-seven.

1917 June: *The Immigrant* is released.

1918 Jan: Chaplin starts filming *A Dog's Life* using artificial lights for the first time.
Oct: *Shoulder Arms* is released – a month before the World War I armistice.
Oct 23: Charles Chaplin, aged twenty-nine, and Mildred Harris are married.

1919 With Douglas Fairbanks and Mary Pickford, Charlie forms the film company, United Artists.

1920 Nov: Charles Chaplin and Mildred Harris are divorced.

1921 *The Kid* is released.
Charlie's mother, Hannah, comes to live in the United States.

1923 Charlie addresses the American Child Health Association.

1924 Charles Chaplin, aged thirty-five, marries Lita Grey.

1925 Charles Spencer Chaplin Junior is born to Charles and Lita. *The Gold Rush* is released.

1926 Charles' and Lita's second son, Sydney Earle Chaplin, is born.

1927 Lita Grey is granted a divorce.

1936 Charles, forty-seven years old, marries Paulette Goddard.

1938 Charlie begins work on *The Great Dictator* which is released in 1940.

1939 Sept: World War II breaks out.

1941 Dec 7: The United States join World War II.

1942 Charles Chaplin and Paulette Goddard are divorced. Charlie meets Oona O'Neill.

1943 June 16: Charlie and Oona are married; she is eighteen and he is fifty-four.

1944 Aug: The first of eight children is born, a daughter Geraldine.

1945 Jan: Charlie makes *Monsieur Verdoux*, the first film in which he speaks.

1947 Charles Chaplin is accused of un-American activities and of being a communist.

1952 Charlie is exiled from America.

1953 Jan: The Chaplin family move to Corsier-sur-Vevey, Switzerland.

1954 May: Charlie is awarded the World Peace Council Prize – he gives the prize money to the poor of Paris and London.

1962 Christopher Chaplin is born to complete the family of eight – Geraldine, Michael, Josephine, Victoria, Eugene, Annette and Jane. Charlie is awarded honorary doctorates at Oxford and Durham Universities, England.

1971 Paris awards Chaplin the "Grande Medaille de Vermail".

1972 America rediscovers Chaplin; his name is added to the Los Angeles "Walk of Fame" and he receives a special Academy Award.

1975 March 4: Charlie is knighted by Queen Elizabeth II.

1977 Dec 25: After making over eighty films, Sir Charles Chaplin dies in his sleep, aged eighty-eight.

Further Reading

Chaplin, Charles: *My Autobiography* (Penguin Books, London, 1987). Charlie remembers his childhood in London and life in America. Fairly light reading – the early chapters on Victorian London are especially interesting historically.

Robinson, David: *Chaplin: His Life and Art* (Paladin Books, London, 1986). An adult book which is long and detailed but full of facts and easy to read.

My Life in Pictures (First published by The Bodley Head, London, 1974, also published in 1985 by Peerage Books). A large book full of pictures of Charlie Chaplin, with his own captions written beside each one.

Films to watch

The Kid – Charles Chaplin *(Tramp)*, Jackie Coogan *(The Kid)*. Released in 1921 but still popular and a classic.

Gold Rush – Charles Chaplin *(Lone Prospector)*, Georgia Hale *(Georgia)*. Released in 1925 this is high comedy and Charlie comes through the winner despite his poor beginnings. Said to be the film Charles Chaplin wished to be remembered by.

City Lights – Charles Chaplin *(The Tramp)*, Virginia Cherrill *(The Blind Girl)*. Released in 1931 this film is both happy and sad; the Tramp is both loser and winner again.

Index